I have often heard people say that they worship the same God Abraham worshipped, or the same God the prophet Moses worshipped. However, some follow [illegible] me are Muslims, and others are Roman Cathol[illegible] f Abraham, and yet I am none of th[illegible] in the writings of the p[illegible] am, and I agree with t[illegible] n the gospel of the Lor[illegible]

Neverthe[illegible] rship the God of Abraham it can be a li[illegible]

It can be compared to a gathering of the Smith family. In many families there is more than one person with the same name. Someone could come to the gathering expecting to see the John Smith they know, but be introduced to someone completely different in looks, age and character. The reason for the error is that two people have been given the same name, but they are not the same person.

Does everyone who claims to worship Abraham's God really worship Him?

Is this true with everyone who says that the God they worship is the same God that Abraham worshipped? Because there can only be one true God, this is important. Jews, Christians and Muslims all claim to serve the God of Abraham, yet their understanding of Him is very different from each other. No two of them can be right.

Some say it doesn't matter. Their attitude is that although they feel they have the truest understanding of who God is, they suppose God will still accept those who have a less perfect grasp of who He is. They believe that although they understand best how God expects them to live, He would never exclude those who live in a different way or have a different approach to worship.

However, most followers of these religions say that it does matter what you believe about God, and they put this into practice. They say that God cares what people believe about Him and how people worship and live. Based on this, some of them banish anyone in their families who change their religion. Others punish them, and some would even kill those who change the belief of their family, country, culture or tradition. This has happened in history and it happens now. Jesus made absolute claims about Himself. He said, "I am the way, the truth and the life, no one comes to the Father, except through Me." (John 14:6)

This question is therefore an important one. If we are to make any headway we have to begin with a few basic questions.

The first is, how can we discover anything about the God of Abraham? The answer is very simple. The oldest documents describing the God of Abraham are the books written by the prophet Moses (Tawrat). The prophets after Moses continued to write about this God. One important thing to recognize about these books is that they have been preserved by the Jews, not the Christians. If Christians tried to change their content Jewish scholars and historians would immediately object and show the world where the changes were. The Jews had such a respect for every letter of the inspired writing that they counted the letters in every line and the number of lines on each section of the scroll as they copied it. Others checked and double checked. Any mistakes resulted in the manuscript being rejected, buried and not used. Because of this, we know that the documents we use today are accurate copies of the documents the former prophets wrote, that Jesus used, and that those who say they follow the God of Abraham or the God of Moses can use with confidence today. This is relevant because it means that we can check any claims about God, by these writings.

Does God change?

There is one question which we will all probably answer in the same way: has God changed? Is God evolving? Has He changed His name? Has He changed in His nature? Has He changed in what He is like or what He likes? Did He accept and forgive sinners in one way previously, and a different way now?

Most of us know that we cannot live up to the standards of God. We don't even live up to our own standards, even though they are very much lower than those God requires. So the question, **"Has God changed?"** is important, because it is linked with the question, "Has He changed in the way He deals with sin?" "Has He changed in the way He accepts people into heaven?" The answer is no! God revealed to one of the former prophets, "I am the Lord, I change not." (Malachi 3:6)

How does Moses describe the God of Abraham?

It is time for us to look at the writings of Moses, because he recorded the life of Abraham for us, and he told us about Abraham's God.

According to Moses, the God of Abraham was not an idol.

Moses wrote that Abraham was born and grew up in Ur, which was part of modern day Iraq. (Genesis 11:28) Abram, as he was then called, was taken by his father Terah to Haran, where they lived. (Genesis 11:31) From there Abraham came into the Land of Canaan.

Moses also indicates that God had revealed Himself to Abraham and had commanded him to leave Ur with all his relatives to go to a land he had never seen, and that there God would make him into a great nation. (Genesis 12:1-2) He said that anyone who was a blessing to Abraham would be blessed and that anyone who troubled him would be troubled by God. God then told him that he would be a means of blessing to all the families of the earth. (Genesis 12:3) Moses recorded the words of God to Abraham, and that He had brought him out of Ur in order to give him that land as an inheritance.

When Abraham arrived in Canaan, he built an altar (a place where a sacrifice was offered) to God, Who, as Moses wrote, had appeared to him and promised to give him the land. Although Abraham built an altar on which to offer sacrifices, he never built an idol. (Genesis 12:7)

From this it is evident that Abraham had left behind the culture he had lived in with all its worship of idols and only worshipped the invisible and eternal God. In Ur, for instance, there were ziggurats and the worship of a moon god. But Abraham, who had lived among those who worshipped using idols of the moon god, never worshipped before a statue or image of a god.

According to Moses, the God of Abraham had a personal name.

People sometimes ask, "What's in a name?" Children are sometimes given names just because some footballer or rock star has that name. In the writings of Moses, names were far more important. A name represented the true nature of a thing. Abram meant 'Exalted Father'. This was interesting, especially as he had no children for many years! However Moses records how God changed Abram's name to Abraham. (Genesis 17:5) This name meant "Father of a multitude" because God said that Abraham, who still had no children, would be the father of many nations.

In the English translation of the Bible, often you will see the name of God written as Lord. The Hebrew word is יהוה , which in English letters is YHWH, and is normally pronounced 'Jehovah'. It means "I AM."

Some names are like titles. For instance we speak of the Queen or the Prime Minister. When we speak to them we might say, "Your Majesty," or "Prime Minister." We are not using their personal name, but a title. The word 'God' is not a personal name. The one Abraham worshipped was not a god, but the only true and living God. And God revealed that He had a personal name.

When Moses or Abraham referred to God by His name, they called Him 'I AM.' It was a name which conveyed a special meaning. It indicates that God exists, and exists eternally and does not need anything or anyone outside of Himself. This is the name that Moses, Abraham, David and all the prophets before Christ used when they referred to God by His personal name. God explained the meaning of His name when He revealed Himself to Moses at the burning bush. Moses was concerned that when people asked him which God had sent him, he would not know what to say. It was then that God clearly stated and explained His name, and told Moses to say, "I AM has sent me to you." (Exodus 3:1-15) Moses was told to say, "The Lord God of your fathers, the God of Abraham… has sent me to you." God then added one very important statement: "this is My name for ever." (Exodus 3:15) Not only does God never change, neither, according to Moses, does His name.

For a mere man to use God's special name for himself would be unthinkable. In fact, it would be considered blasphemy. That is why there was uproar when Jesus said the words, "Before Abraham was, I am." (Read John 8:51-59) He did not say, "Before Abraham was, I was." That would have been startling enough. He had just been asked by the Jews how He could have seen Abraham when He was less than fifty years old Himself. He could have said, "Before Abraham existed, I existed." Even that would have implied that He was claiming to be divine. Instead, He chose His words carefully, and said something that the Jews could not possibly misunderstand. The people listening knew that Jesus was taking the name of the God of Abraham and making it His very own name, so they immediately tried to kill Him for blasphemy. He did not try to correct them.

The main point is this. The God of Abraham had a personal name. Moses and the former prophets only referred to God by this name, and God said to Moses that this was His only name for ever. It was Jehovah, I AM, and is translated into the English Bible by the word LORD.

According to Moses, the God of Abraham was the creator of the Universe.

Moses wrote about the creation of the world. In Genesis chapters 1 to 11 we read of the history of the world before Abraham was born.

Moses wrote that the creation of the whole universe was completed in six days. (Genesis 1) He described the sin of Adam (Genesis 3). He showed how Adam's sin separated him from fellowship with God, and how all Adam's descendents inherit his sinful nature, and are themselves born already separated from God and under His judgment. Then Moses recorded God promising to send a Saviour who would be wounded as He crushed Satan and through His death would restore the relationship between believers and God by forgiving all their sin and changing their sinful hearts. (Genesis 3:15) Moses' record of history continued as Abel offered a sacrifice to be accepted with

God. Later, God brought the flood on the world. The evidence for this flood is everywhere over the face of the world.

So Moses had described the creator God, who promised to send a Saviour and who judged the world. After the flood Noah was thankful. However, he did not merely say a prayer of thanks, but he too offered a sacrifice on an altar.

Noah's sons were still alive when Abraham, who was a descendent of Shem, was born. Moses made clear that Abraham was a worshipper of the same creator God who promised the Messiah. There is one incident which makes this clear. You can read it in Genesis 14.

When Abraham rescued his nephew Lot from king Chedorlaomer, the prophet Moses recorded the incident where Melchizedek, who was a priest and worshipper of the one true God, came out to meet him with both bread and wine. (Genesis 14:17-18) Melchizedek said that Abraham had been blessed by "the most high God, possessor of heaven and earth." (Genesis 14:19) Abraham responded to this by saying, "I have lifted up my hand unto the Lord, the most high God, the possessor of heaven and earth…" (Genesis 14:22) Abraham used the personal name of God. He said that the God who possesses the whole universe is the God whose name is Jehovah, which, of course, means I AM.

According to Moses, the God of Abraham appeared to Abraham in the form of a man.

Later in Abraham's life, Moses described a meeting between the

Lord and Abraham. Abraham was sitting in his tent doorway in the middle of the day when God appeared. (Genesis 15:1) There were three men, and one of them gave the promise that Sarah would have a son. (Genesis 18:9-12) When Sarah laughed with disbelief, Moses wrote that it was the Lord who rebuked her. The Lord then informed Abraham that He would destroy the wicked cities of Sodom and Gomorrah. After Abraham finished asking the Lord for mercy for the cities, it tells us that the Lord 'went His way' and that only two persons went to Sodom. Therefore Moses had no difficulty writing the incident to reveal to us that just as two angels had appeared in the form of men, so the Lord had also appeared in the form of a man to Abraham. (Genesis 18:31-19:1)

We all believe God could do anything. He could become man without ceasing to be God. The great questions we have to address are: whether He has done this, and if so, why? Moses recorded this incident where three persons, who were called men, appeared before Abraham. Two went to Sodom, and Moses wrote that they were angels. Abraham stood before one of them and Abraham called him "the Lord," (Genesis 18:27) meaning 'I AM'. Therefore, as far as Moses was concerned, who recorded this incident, the God of Abraham took the form of a man to speak with Abraham.

So those who worship the God of Abraham should have no difficulty believing that God could, would and did become man without ceasing to be God.

According to Moses, the God of Abraham accepted Abraham when he believed his promise

The question of how we can be right with God is important. There are those who use their religion like a shield. Often when I speak to people they will say, "Oh! I am a Roman Catholic." In other words, "I'm OK." Some may think because they have been through a ceremony in a church as a baby, or were born into a Muslim home, or have learned a Bible verse, or the Koran, then all is well.

They believe one of two things. Either they think that because something was done to them or that something was done by them as a member of their religion, God will accept them. For instance, a person may have been christened or circumcised and think that makes them right with God. Or they feel that doing good things or going on pilgrimage, will make amends for their sins and guarantee their place in Paradise.

How was Abraham accepted before God? Moses tells us. The Lord appeared to Abraham in a vision (Genesis 15:1). Abraham believed that God would send a Saviour who would take the place of sinners and be punished as a sacrifice in their place. This was the promise given to Adam. When God appeared to Abraham, He promised that those who would descend from Abraham spiritually would be more numerous than could be counted. God was not emphasising that Abraham's descendents would be the children of his body, but of his belief in the Saviour. We are told by Moses that Abraham believed this promise and put his trust in the Lord. Then Moses recorded the words that the Lord 'accounted it to him for righteousness.' (Genesis 15:6) Before any ceremony of circumcision had begun, and without Abraham having to do anything to make amends for the sins he had committed, he put his trust in the Lord and was counted as right with God.

Most religions say that if you want to be forgiven or to be sure of acceptance with God you must do something to make up for your sins. The God of Abraham never asked Abraham for this. He made a promise and Abraham put his trust in the promise. From that moment on, Abraham was counted as righteous.

The way Abraham was declared right with God by trusting God's promise is exactly the way Christians are declared right with God. They believe the promise that God would send and has sent the Saviour. My Muslim friends have often said to me that if people are forgiven just by believing in Jesus, then they could go and commit any sins they want to. They are forgetting that Abraham was counted right with God in exactly this way, but he did not then live a wicked life. Christians call this being 'justified by faith,' because the Gospel describes it in these words. It is as if we have gone into God's courtroom accused of all our sins, but He has declared that those sins are not placed on our charge sheet. Instead, we are counted as having been perfectly good. Faith is trusting that the promise made by God is enough, and through believing that promise God will keep His word and forgive all our sins. We do not have to go on pilgrimages, keep fasts and give alms to earn salvation, instead the God of Abraham has promised to provide a remedy for sin for those who repent and place their trust in that promise. All those who are justified in this way, go on to live a righteous life, as Abraham did.

According to Moses, the God of Abraham promised to bless the whole world through sending a Son of Abraham into the world.

In the Tawrat (Genesis 3:15), Moses recorded the promise that God would send someone who would put right what Satan had made wrong when he tempted Adam and Eve to rebelled against God. The promised Saviour would provide forgiveness and also restore the believer's relationship with God. Throughout the Old Testament this person is described. His place of birth would be Bethlehem. (Micah 5:2) He would be a descendent of the prophet and king, David. (Isaiah 11:1-5; Jeremiah 23:5-6) The prophets described him so clearly that anyone reading their descriptions would be tempted to think that those writers lived after Jesus was born rather than many hundreds of years before he came into the world. The description of the Jews rejecting Him, giving Him a false trial and many other specific incidents at the time of His trial and death were prophesied in great detail in the writings of the former prophets, called the Old Testament. In particular, the prophet David described a crucifixion scene in Psalm 22, hundreds of years before the Romans devised that form of execution, and 1000 years before Jesus was born. Later, about 600 years before Jesus was born, the prophet Isaiah described the day of the crucifixion in Isaiah 53.

The point I am making is that Abraham believed that God would send that Saviour. True believers—including Abraham—right up to the coming of Jesus, looked forward in time and believed that this Saviour, called the Messiah, would come. They were trusting in the Messiah, even though He had not yet been born. Those who are real Christians have exactly the same faith as those believers before Jesus came. The only difference is that they look back in time and see that God did send the Saviour who dealt with sin by living as they ought to have lived, and then dying as they deserved to die.

Moses not only recorded the first promise of God to send a Saviour, he revealed that the promised Saviour would be a descendent of Abraham. (Genesis 22:18)

According to Moses, the God of Abraham accepted people through the death of a substitute which died instead of them.

Throughout Abraham's life he erected altars on which he offered sacrifices, but he did not make idols. Moses had already written that Abel, Adam's son offered a sacrifice of a lamb and was accepted before God. Moses also recorded that Noah offered a sacrifice after the flood. Moses wrote many times about the meaning of sacrifices. On each occasion the reason for the sacrifice was that a sinful person came to worship the LORD, but before he could worship acceptably, the lamb or other sacrifice had to die instead of him. It was as if he looked at the animal as it died and was burnt to ashes, and thought, "I deserve that. I deserve to die and to go to hell fire for my sins, but I am alive because the sacrifice died in my place." Moses wrote one complete book about the meaning of sacrifices. It is called Leviticus. In that book, Moses emphasised repeatedly that the sacrifices had to be perfect and without blemish.

It is this concept of altars for offering a sacrifice for sin that helps us understand the occasion when God tested Abraham. (Genesis 22:1) He took the son he loved and went to Mount Moriah where God said Abraham should offer him as a burnt offering. (Genesis 22:2) Abraham obeyed God. As they walked, Abraham's son asked a question. "My father, look, the fire and wood, but where is the lamb for a burnt offering?" Moses recorded that Abraham's son knew that if they were going to worship God, they would need to offer a sacrifice. It would have to die and be burnt to ashes if they were to be accepted. Abraham replied that God Himself would provide the lamb for the burnt offering. (Genesis 22:8) In the Injil we learn that Abraham supposed that even if he had to go through with the offering, and kill his own son, God would raise him from the dead, so that God's promises to bless the world and bring the Messiah into the world through his son, could still be fulfilled.

When Abraham was about to kill his son, God stopped him. God did not say, "You have passed the test, so now you can go home." Instead, God provided a ram. In the place of his son, the ram was offered as a burnt offering. It is only in true Christianity that this makes sense. The New Testament agrees with Moses that before sinful men can be accepted before a holy God, there is a need for a sacrifice. That sacrifice has to die so that the sinner can be accepted. This is the purpose of the Messiah coming. John the Baptist pointed to Jesus and said to the people, "See, the Lamb of God who takes away the sin of the world."(John 1:29)

So, according to Moses, the God of Abraham accepts sinners only through the death of a perfect substitute. The Gospel shows that the lambs offered before Jesus died were a picture of Jesus the Messiah. It is only because He died as a sinless sacrifice and substitute that we as sinners can be accepted before the holy God of Abraham.

But what does the gospel, (the Injil) say about the God of Abraham?

Everything I have discussed so far is from the prophet Moses, but the New Testament of the Holy Bible continues to describe the God of Abraham. Of interest to us is that nowhere in the New Testament does anything change. Of particular importance is how Jesus referred to Abraham's God, and especially how He spoke to the Jews of His day who were hostile to Him.

But why is this so important? The answer is simple. You may believe you are worshipping and serving the God of Abraham, when you may not be. Your god may be a totally different person. I am not saying that there is more than one God. There is only one God, and if we are not worshipping the one true and living God then we are not worshipping God at all, but are worshipping something which someone has made up in their imagination.

So let us explore what the Gospel says about God and see if He is the same God as the prophet Moses described.

1. The New Testament teaches that God is not an idol.

First, the New Testament, including Jesus, declares that God is not to be worshipped through idols. "No one has seen God at any time," said John in the Gospel which he wrote. (John 1:18) Jesus said "God is Spirit, and those who worship Him must worship Him in spirit and truth." (John 4:24) Those who make statues, especially of Mary or Jesus, are going against what Jesus himself said.

2. The New Testament teaches that the name of God is Jehovah.

Jesus referred to the name of God exactly as Moses did. Remember that the name of God was Jehovah, which meant "I AM". A situation arose where the Jews accused Jesus of being possessed by a devil because He said that if a man kept what He said that man would live forever." (John 8:51) They said that Abraham and the other prophets were all dead, and asked if Jesus was greater than those former prophets. (John 8:52-53) They asked Him, "Who do you think you are?" (John 8:53) His reply was firstly to say that if He said He did not know God, He would be a liar, just as they were, because they said they did know God, when they did not. (verse 55) He then said that Abraham was looking forward to seeing the day when Christ would come. This was too much for the Jews. They said that Jesus wasn't 50 years old, so how could He have seen Abraham. The response of Jesus is remarkable. He said, "Before Abraham was I AM." He took the name of Abraham's God as His own name. He did not say, "Before Abraham was, I was." Instead He took the only name of God as His own.

Whatever else this indicates, it proves again that God's name is Jehovah, I AM.

3. The New Testament teaches that God is the Most High God, the Creator.

The New Testament agrees that this great God is also the creator, controller and king of the Universe. In one letter, the account of Abraham's meeting with Melchizedek is repeated and He is again called the Most High God. (Hebrews 7:1) The first Christian to be martyred was murdered as he spoke of the God of Moses and David also spoke of God as the Most High who does not dwell in a temple. (Acts 7:46)

4. The New Testament teaches that God came into the world as a man.

Fourthly, the New Testament continues to show that God not only appeared as a man, but came as a man to deal with the sin of man. John, a relative and disciple of Jesus, wrote "In the beginning was the Word, and the Word was with God and the Word was God." (John 1:1) He said that everything was made by Him and without Him nothing that exists came into being. Yet he later wrote, "And the Word was made flesh and dwelt among us." (John 1:14) John was explaining that the person called the Word was Jesus Christ. (Also see 1 Timothy 3:16)

The God who appeared as man to Abraham, as Moses recorded, came into the world, as John recorded. Jesus made clear that He was the Son of God. Many times He said this and the Jews understood perfectly what He meant. In John 10:33 they accused Jesus of blasphemy for calling Himself the Son of God. They said specifically that they intended to stone Him because He, though a man was making Himself God. (John 10:33) In fact, the final reason that Jesus was put on the Cross was for blasphemy. They asked if He really was the Son of the Blessed God, and He said categorically "I am." (Mark 14:61-62) There is no doubt that the Jews understood this as people today do. Anyone claiming to be the Son of God is claiming to be a divine person. Jesus was claiming to be both God and man. He was God appearing in human form, just as the God of Abraham did 2000 years before Jesus was born.

5. The New Testament teaches that salvation is by faith in the promise of God.

I wrote earlier that the God of Abraham declared that Abraham was right with Him, not because Abraham did some great or good thing, nor because he went on pilgrimage or became a martyr, but because Abraham believed the promise given to him.

Jesus very specially repeats that this is the way that anyone is accepted with God. When a very religious and upright person came to discuss salvation with Jesus one evening, Jesus stopped any discussion by declaring that "God so loved the world that He gave His only begotten Son that whoever believes in Him should not perish but have everlasting life." (John 3:16) If you think this is not enough and that you need to do something to earn a place in Paradise, Jesus repeated many times that people obtain their place in Paradise by trusting the promises of God and not by trying to do something to make amends for their sins. He said, "He who believes in Him," that is, in the Son of God, "is not condemned; but he who does not believe is condemned already, because he has not believed in the name of the only begotten Son of God." (John 3:18) This is repeated so many times. "He who believes in Me has everlasting life." (John 3:36) On one occasion people asked, "What shall we do, that we might work the works of God?" Jesus did not give a list of two, five or ten things that would be enough to gain acceptance. He replied, "This is the work of God, that you believe in Him whom He sent." (John 6:29) The New Testament is consistent with the words of Moses about Abraham that we are not saved by our good works, but by faith in Christ alone. Speaking to Christians it says, "For it is by grace you have been saved, through faith - and this not from yourselves, it is the gift of God - not by works, so that no-one can boast." (Ephesians 2:8-9)

6. The New Testament teaches that Jesus is the one promised by the God of Abraham who would bless the world.

God had promised to bless the world by sending a son of Abraham into the world, but was Jesus that person? Jesus certainly said so, when He said that His hearers were searching the scriptures, but could not see that those writings spoke about Him. (John 5.39) A few sentences later Jesus said clearly that the people who were opposing Him thought they were trusting in Moses, but that Moses himself would accuse them on the judgment day. He then told them why. He said, "if you believed Moses, you would believe Me; because he wrote about Me." (John 5:46) Again, the New Testament states very clearly that all the former prophets were prophesying that forgiveness of sins would be obtained through the coming Messiah, Jesus. (Acts 10:43)

The Gospel of Matthew opens with these words, "The book of the generation of Jesus Christ, the son of David, the son of Abraham." (Matthew 1:1) And the gospel of Luke records the lineage of Jesus from Adam, through Abraham and the prophet David. (Luke 3:23-38) There can be no doubt that Jesus knew that He was the one promised to bless the world as the descendent of Abraham. He said that people were searching the Scriptures for eternal life, but that the Scriptures spoke about Him. (John 5:39) This is a remarkable claim.

7. The New Testament teaches that God accepted the death of Christ as the sacrifice for sin.

The prophet Moses wrote how God accepted a sacrifice instead of punishing the sinner and the New Testament continues to teach this truth. The prophet, John the Baptist, called Jesus 'The Lamb of God who takes away the sin of the world.' (John 1:29) Other Old Testament prophets described the death of the Messiah, but both David and Isaiah were the most specific. If you read Psalm 22 which was written 1000 years before the Messiah was born, you will be amazed to read how He would die. If you read Isaiah chapter 53, it is equally amazing to read why He would die. In that prophecy it is clear that the Lord would lay on Him the iniquity of us all, (Isaiah 53:6) and that "He poured out His soul unto death, And He was numbered with the transgressors, And He bore the sin of many." (Isaiah 53:12) Jesus said, "Therefore My Father loves Me, because I lay down My life that I may take it again. No one takes it from Me, but I lay it down of Myself. I have power to lay it down, and I have power to take it again. This command I have received from My Father." (John 10:17-18)

It is evident therefore that just as God accepted people because of the sacrifice of a lamb in the Old Testament, so Christ was the Lamb who had come to die so that others could be forgiven.

Moses and the Gospel are in agreement.

The Old and New Testaments are the two lips of the one mouth of God. They both say the same things. The God of Abraham that

Moses so clearly described is the God of the New Testament of the Bible.

It is easy to say that you worship the God of Abraham, but do you worship the God that Moses described? Do you worship the invisible, infinite and eternal God, whose name is I AM (Jehovah), the Creator of the Universe, who came into the world as a man without ceasing to be God? Do you worship the God who accepts sinners, not because of any ceremony they go through, or any good thing they do to make amends for their sin, but only by faith as they trust in His promises to forgive freely? Do you believe in the God who promised to send the Messiah from among Abraham's children? Do you believe in that Messiah who died as a sinless substitute and sacrifice in the place of the sinner.

Conclusion

In the days of Jesus many people claimed to worship the same God Abraham worshipped, but Jesus said that they were not worshipping Him. They said they were the descendants of Abraham, but Jesus said they were not. Who then are the real descendants of Abraham, and who are the true worshippers of Abraham's God? When people said to Jesus, "Abraham is our father." Jesus said to them, "If you were Abraham's children, you would do the works of Abraham. But now you seek to kill Me, a Man who has told you the truth which I heard from God. Abraham did not do this. You do the deeds of your father." Then they said to Him, "We were not born of fornication; we have one Father—God." (John 8:39-41) It is evident at this point that they assume that the God of Abraham is the God they are worshipping and serving, but notice now how Jesus responded, "If God were your Father, you would love Me, for I proceeded forth and came from God; nor have I come of Myself, but He sent Me." (John 8:42)

On one occasion Jesus said to His opponents, "You are from beneath; I am from above. You are of this world; I am not of this world. Therefore I said to you that you will die in your sins; for if you do not believe that I am, you will die in your sins." (John 8:23-24) There is no wonder that the astonished hearers asked, "Who are you?" (John 8:25) He was making a claim that resulted in His being crucified for blasphemy.

This is the point I have been coming to. If the God of Abraham is really the God you worship and serve, you would love Jesus Christ who came forth from God. You would believe that God's name is Jehovah, that He is the creator of all things and that He appears as a man and accepts those who put their trust in Him rather than in their own goodness. They believe that they are accepted because God has accepted Christ's sacrifice as He died on the cross on their behalf.

Many, in the days when Jesus lived, supposed they were right and were worshipping the God of Abraham but they were not. It is exactly the same today. Remember the words of Jesus. May you turn to Him rather than experience what He said to His critics 2000 years ago;

"Do not think that I shall accuse you to the Father; there is one who accuses you—Moses, in whom you trust. For if you believed Moses, you would believe Me; for he wrote about Me. But if you do not believe his writings, how will you believe My words?" (John 5:45-47)